Soul on Rice

Soul on Rice

Patricia B. Mitchell

With Bibliographical Notes

Copyright © 1993 by Patricia B. Mitchell. All rights reserved.

Published 1993 by the author.

Mail: Mitchells, P.O. Box 429, Chatham, VA 24531

FoodHistory.com and *MitchellsPublications.com*

Book Sales: 800-967-2867

E-mail: *Answers@FoodHistory.com*

Bookshelf Edition

ISBN-13: 978-1981101290

First printing, January 2018

Illustrations

Front cover – Drawing by Mary Hallock Foote, published in *Harper's Weekly*, December 28, 1878. Background image, "Solely Rice," adapted from a photograph by Henry H. Mitchell, *HenryHMitchell.com*. Border inspired by a coverlet woven by a slave named Booker, Shady Grove Plantation (once owned by the Stone family), Sheva, Pittsylvania County, Virginia, early 1800s.

Inside title page – Provided by Dover Publications, Inc.

Back cover – "Maspero's Entresol, Circa 1840," a mixed-media drawing, © 1974 by Robert C. Adler, first published in the February 1975 issue of *The Community Standard Monthly Awards Magazine*. The drawing depicts a slave awaiting sale at Maspero's Slave Exchange (now a restaurant), Chartres and St. Louis Streets, New Orleans, Louisiana.

Graphic research and design are by Sarah E. Mitchell, *VintageDesigns.com*.

"Some sat in darkness and the deepest gloom, prisoners suffering in iron chains. . . . Then they cried to the Lord in their trouble, and he saved them from their distress. He brought them out of darkness and the deepest gloom and broke away their chains."

- Psalms 107:10, 13, 14

A Note of Appreciation from the Author

. . . To the staff of the Pittsylvania County (Virginia) Public Library for their research assistance.

Table of Contents

Introduction 1

Chapter 1: African Foodways 3

Chapter 2: Shackled............................11

Chapter 3: Making a Home Away from Home 16

Chapter 4: "Our T' Eat" 40

Notes 96

Index..111

Introduction

As Nzingha Dalila, now a resident of Cincinnati, Ohio, but originally from Angola, pointed out, "[Slaves] were forced to eat things they wouldn't have, if they'd had a choice." [1] This book is about how black people adapted to the foods in America, and the circumstances in which they found themselves as slaves on foreign soil. Slaves took inferior rations and dire situations and made the best of them. Gumbos, cornbreads, and chitterlings demonstrate such culinary successes. Black resiliency demonstrates personal and cultural victories.

The half million Africans surviving the formidable passage across the Atlantic to America brought virtually no material possessions with them. However, they did bring something of even greater value: a rich cultural heritage. Native African foodways were an important part of this legacy. The diet of the average population in Africa centered around cultivated plant foods — starchy grains, roots, and legumes. Rice was a much-used food; and maize, introduced to West African regions in the 16th century, became a staple. Sorghum (or "guinea corn"), millet, yams, groundnuts (akin to the peanut), and cowpeas (called "black-eyed" peas in this country) were essential to the diet. Green leafy vegetables, okra, varieties of pumpkins, squashes, gourds, and cucumbers were eaten. Eggplant, introduced there prior to the Middle Ages by Arab and Persian travelers, was cultivated. Fruits and meats were secondary components of the typical diet in West Africa,[2] the area from which most slaves came.

The purpose of this book is to further investigate native African food customs and how they changed in a new environment, and to document African influences on American foodways.

Chapter 1: African Foodways

Generally speaking, it can be restated that among the people of West Africa, food of a vegetable origin comprised a major part of the daily fare. However, in the past, wealthy tribal chiefs and notables ate more meat than the common man. Also, among the minority of peoples who primarily hunted and fished, meat and fish made up the bulk of the diet; and among pastoralists (those with flocks), meat was a vital element of the diet.[3] Most of the population, though, were agriculturalists, with a diet which would be considered by modern nutritionists as very healthful: little meat, lots of vegetables, and high fiber.

Grains such as millet (called *dukhn*) and a kind of wheat were used, as well as rice and sorghum. These grainstuffs were made into pancakes, fritters, breads, thick porridges, and assorted puddings served with a variety of sauces.

Kidney beans, cowpeas (black-eyed peas), broad beans (*Vicia faba*), chickpeas (garbanzos), and lentils were consumed;[4] as were lima beans and Congo beans or pigeon beans.[5] Yams (*Dioscorea*) were (and are) an important component of the diet.[6] In fact, the word "yam" comes from the West African verb "to eat" — *njam, nyami,* or *djambi.*[7]

In the old days in Mali, on the West Coast of Africa, a festival at yam harvest time was associated with the symbolic and extremely culturally significant blood-sacrifice of a man. The blood sacrifice was offered in order to ensure crop fertility. Historians believe that a criminal was executed by order of a tribal king. This sacrifice, by beheading, took place in the yam field on the fifth day of the yam celebration. The human sacrifice was thought to go forth as a messenger to the most-recently-deceased king. The convict was killed and his blood allowed to flow into the hole from which a fresh yam had just been extracted. The reigning king, at this point, could partake of the new crop.

His subjects, too, feasted.[8] The absolute prohibition of the eating of the new crop before the proper ceremony was taken so seriously that there are documented cases of prisoners starving to death voluntarily rather than eat yams because they did not know whether "New Yam" had been eaten in their home villages.[9] Some writers also assert that cannibalism of the human sacrifice occurred at the time of the New Yam Festival. Other African superstitions associated with yams have included the idea that the first solid food consumed by an infant should be yams. Special types of foods prepared with yams are also served at the naming ceremony of a child, and at funerals. It is considered unsafe to sleep in a room in which yams are kept. It is also believed that at night, stored yams hum to each other. Stealing yams was viewed as an extremely serious crime; and committing adultery in a yam field is a criminal offense, according to Ibo traditional law. (Adultery occurring elsewhere was a civil offense.)[10]

Yams were thought of as symbols of human fertility among the tribes of Nigeria

(Ibo, Yoruba, etc.). They also used yams in much the same way that we use money. Therefore, to them, yams represented wealth. As a foodstuff, boiled yams (and other starchy foods such as cassava, rice, or plantains) were often pounded to a glutenous mass and utilized in the coastal Guinea version of *fufu*, a traditional dish. The cook used a huge mortar and pestle to mash the tubers to the consistency of dumpling dough. Over this bland base a sauce was served. Yams were also served after being boiled or roasted with their skins on. Sometimes they were cooked with pieces of chicken or ram's meat. — Sweet potatoes were also prepared either boiled or roasted.[11]

(The American sweet potato, botanically an entirely different plant from the yam, was introduced to Africa in the 16th century, as was maize.[12] Christopher Columbus first encountered the sweet potato in 1492 in Hispañola [now Cuba and the Dominican Republic]. The tuber rapidly became a staple food on board ships in the

Atlantic trade, and subsequently edged its way into Old World cookery.[13])

After the Columbian exchange (when New World foods were taken to Europe and Africa), varieties of hot peppers were enjoyed by Africans. Cassava, white potatoes, tomatoes, maize, coconut, and pineapple were all introduced to Africa between 1520 and 1540. — Many types of green leafy vegetables and herbs were cultivated in Africa. Spinach, bitterleaf, and okra, which are indigenous to Africa, were planted. Members of the onion family were grown. Seeds and nuts were important foods. Sesame seeds (originally from the Orient), pistachios, hazelnuts, groundnuts, cucumber and melon seeds added protein and diverse flavors to the diet. Watermelon was a favorite food. Bosman, a Dutchman who traveled along the coast of Guinea in the 1700s, noted:

> "[Ripe watermelons are] delicious, watery, refreshing, cooling . . . . They are twice as big as our melons . . . . When green it is eaten

as a salad, instead of cucumbers, to which it is not wholly unlike." [14]

Ackee, plums, dates, figs, tamarind, star apples, fig bananas, plantains, pomegranates, and other fruits were eaten by Africans.

Palm oil, shea butter (an African vegetable butter made from the fruit of the *Butyrospermum parkii* tree), sesame oil, butter and animal fat, coconut oil (and coconut milk) were part of the diet depending upon the African locality. (The coconut tree was introduced to West Africa between 1520 and 1540. This plant came from southern Asia and the East African coast.)[15] When available, beef, camel, goat, lamb, pork, poultry, and varieties of game and fish were usually consumed boiled, grilled, or roasted. Meat was sun-dried, smoked, corned, or salted for preservation. By the 16th century pork was "esteemed a great delicacy" in West Africa. (Those of Islamic faith did not consume pork, however.) Roasted meats were frequently served with a sauce, such a dish being the forerunner of modern barbecue.[16]

In West Africa grilled or fried chicken was usually served with a sauce over rice or other starchy base. Guinea hens and chickens were raised by West African families for use as food or for trade,[17] but consumption of such birds was ofttimes a "special occasion" occurrence; and some tribes permitted only women and children to eat poultry and eggs. For adult men such foods were taboo.[18]

In Africa, as in most ancient cultures, women did the cooking. (And, in West African villages, they often controlled the granary, the food storage area. The females also sold in local and regional markets surplus crops which they had harvested.[19])

A vegetable stew served with a "mash" such as *fufu* or rice was the typical fare. Even today *fouto*, made with okra and green peppers, is considered the "national stew" of the Guineans.[20] Two meals were eaten per day, one at noon and one in the evening, although having a piece of fruit or bread as a "snack" was common.[21] When desserts were prepared, puddings made from "intensely sweet" plump fig bananas were well-liked. African cooks also used cormantyn apples, custard apples, yams and sweet potatoes, etc. for pudding concoctions. Some West African women also sold homemade cakes and sugar cane syrup candies in the village market place. The cakes were made from a diversity of ingredients — rice, flour, and coconuts; fermented cassava dough; dried tapioca and grated coconuts; cornmeal, rice, and eggs; beans; wheat flour and eggs; and fried fig bananas.[22]

The mealtime "sauce" or thick soup was well-seasoned, that is to say, hot and spicy, but the base of bland starch counteracted the fieriness. Diners took a small amount of *fufu* in their fingers and used it to scoop up some of the groundnut stew or other entree. Another possible meal presentation was a one-pot combination of stew and rice — jollof rice, for example.[23]

Meats were often considered a "flavor enhancer" rather than the main focus of a dish because of the small quantity of available meat.[24]

African beverages included palm wine, beer made from millet, unfermented beverages thickened with millet or other cereals, honey water, and perhaps mead, fresh and sour milk, and water.[25]

Chapter 2: Shackled

Slavery had been common in Africa and in the rest of the world since ancient times. Enslaved peoples (criminals, debtors, the destitute, war captives) were routinely traded within Africa itself. (However, enslavement did not necessarily last a lifetime because slaves could perhaps buy their freedom or regain it through military service.)

After a passage of time the slave trade escalated. To fill the demand "slave raiding parties" went into the interior to indiscriminately take captives. Demand for slaves was again increased in the mid-15th century when Portuguese explorers began buying African slaves to serve in homes in Portugal. In the 1490s and early 1500s the Portuguese began growing sugar cane on islands off the African coast. Soon they wanted African slaves to work at these sugar plantations. New World colonies followed this example; and in 1518 the first shiploads of black African slaves sailed from West Africa to the West Indies.[26]

    Accounts of voyages across the Atlantic are generally gruesome. "Slavers" were ships fitted out with a hidden slave deck which could hold as many as 750 slaves. The standard plan for such a vessel showed floor space to accommodate several hundred human beings lying down, back to belly "stacked almost like cordwood." [27] Inhumanly crowded conditions, boredom, mediocre food, and sickness made the uprooted people feel even more despondent and fearful of the future. Needless to say, though, the slave merchants wanted the human cargo to survive, because the slaves represented potential profit. In fact, Africans came to be known as "black gold." [28] The slavers (slave dealers as well as slave ships were called "slavers") therefore hired surgeons to inspect slaves, selecting healthy people who would command a good price in America. Blacks were examined to see if they were "physically fit," had "healthy eyes, good teeth," stood "over four feet high, and if men, [were] not ruptured; if women, have not 'fallen breasts' " [29] or, as another description reads, "The Countenance, and Stature, a good Set of Teeth, Pliancy in their Limbs and Joints, and being free of Venereal Taint, are the things inspected and governs our choice in buying." [30]

The doctor checked on the captured people for the months which they might be held on the African coast before they were shipped. Then the surgeon went on the voyage to continue watch over his charges. Each day he examined the slaves; and he was also involved in planning food purchases before the trip and possibly for overseeing feeding during the passage.

Good nutritional practices, even among the ship's crew, were a just-emerging science. The way to prevent scurvy had been hit upon (consumption of fruits and vegetables containing vitamin C), and the benefits of cleanliness were being discovered, but many characteristics of a healthful diet were not well understood. Nevertheless, the slave dealers wanted their unfortunate cargo to appear strong, rather than emaciated, when they reached the auction block.

On most slave vessels the blacks were fed twice daily from large tubs. They were given wooden spoons and the people gathered, about ten to each tub.[31]

The contents of the tub varied, with some consideration being given to the native diet of the particular people being transported. One slave ship staple was mush made of palm oil and maize.[32]

A similar porridge called "slabber-sauce" was made with palm oil, flour, pepper, and water. On English ships dried "horse beans" were boiled with lard to a pulp. Sometimes black-eyed peas were served with rice; rice and yams were used frequently. (Africans from the Windward and Guinea coasts were accustomed to rice; captives from the Bight of Benin normally consumed yams at home, so they were fed them.) On occasion salted fish, fried corn cakes, vegetables, lemons, and limes were given to the slaves; meat was seldom offered. Slavers stated that Africans had "a good stomach" for beans.[33]

Yet the "medical care" and food offered did not prevent death at sea. For every five slaves who arrived alive in the Americas, it is estimated that one died in transit.[34]

Chapter 3: Making a Home Away from Home

The West Indies were often a way station en route to the mainland north of Spanish Florida. Blacks passing through this area perhaps were briefly exposed to the zesty foods of the Creole islanders — foods which were no doubt a blessed relief after the dismal slave ship victuals. Being given fresh vegetables or fruit when arriving in the West Indies (or Cuba) broke the deadening monotony of the captives' diet. Perhaps the Africans got a taste — or at least a whiff — of exuberant dishes like pepper pot, gumbo, and *à la daube* (fish or other food in gelatin). When the Africans finally reached their new American home, the people chosen as cooks quickly began to demonstrate their cooking genius in producing foods which reflected African and Creole (West Indian) tastes while still appealing to the English palate with its Native American borrowings.[35]

The African woman appointed to be the cook in a Southern plantation kitchen reigned over a hot domain, for the cooking was done in a very large fireplace in the kitchen house, a building separate from the "big house." The dominant feature of the kitchen was a fireplace measuring maybe four feet deep, seven feet high, and ten feet wide, containing two sturdy andirons set about six feet apart, for supporting the main fire logs. This wood-eating wonder turned into a blast furnace on windy days, and an aggravation during wet periods when firewood became damp.[36]

The kitchen was built away from the mansion to keep out flies, cooking odors, noise, and heat; and to prevent the main house from burning down if a kitchen fire occurred. The cook and the second cook (her assistant) were aided by black children assigned to carry food "to and fro between kitchen and dining room to supply the butler and maids with hot food for the table . . . [to keep flies off the dining table] with a fly brush made of peacock feathers . . . [to]

run errands, 'tote' water from the spring and . . . whatever they were told." [37]

The cook and her helpers worked at the wide hearth, hanging kettles and pots from pot hooks on the long iron rods (called "cranes") in front of the fireplace. There was also a spit, a long iron rod onto which was impaled a piece of meat or a fowl. This rod or spit was set in front of the fire and rotated constantly as the meat cooked. Often a black child had the job of turning the spit.

Dutch ovens, or deep skillets with legs and lids, were set on hot coals and covered with the coals. In addition there was usually an oven built in the side of the brick fireplace. Breads, cakes, and other foods could be prepared in this oven.

Kitchen tools included a long-handled shovel, bellows to blow the fire, poker and tongs, and spoons, cooking forks, etc. All water had to be drawn from a well or cistern or brought from the spring, then heated in large pots and kettles. There was no sink, so dishes were washed in a large dishpan.[38]

The cooking fire was kept blazing all day and glowing at night, so the kitchen was, especially in the summer, an inferno-like, nonpaying sweatshop. Open-hearth cooking was physically taxing, as well as risky. The cook was constantly lifting heavy pots and stooping, her long skirts and sleeves hanging dangerously close to the flames and embers. Burned arms and fingers were an occupational hazard, and scalded limbs or face could easily happen if a pot dropped or a pothook snapped. A pot of cooking food could be ruined if a glob of soot or caked grease fell into it from an improperly cleaned chimney.[39] Though a house cook earned a certain amount of prestige among her peers, she clearly had an arduous occupation.

A black cook might also be in charge of providing meals for the black population of the plantation. (This might be the same woman who cooked for the white people, or, on the larger plantations, another black cook who cooked exclusively for her fellow slaves.) Breakfasts and (mid-day) dinners were the meals most often prepared in large quantities for distribution to the field hands. The slaves who were fed in this manner worked on an empty stomach from sunrise until around eight a.m., at which time food was brought in buckets or baskets to the field. At noon food was again delivered.

Former slave Levi Pollard reported on his daily meal schedule:

> "Us eat breakfast 'roun eight o'clock. De folks dat was in de fields would cum home or else de ones at home would tote hit [it] ter 'em. Dey go ter work 'round five en six o'clock. Dey ain't eat fo' dey go. Us eat mush en things like dat fo breakfast.
>
> "Dinner was half past twelve or one o'clock. Always nearly have boil dinner, er fried dinner er soup.
>
> "Fur supper most times molasses en bread [corn], er hind en milk, or suppers suppin like dat. Dis was 'round six o'clock.

"After supper us ain't eat no mo 'til de next mornin' at breakfast." [40]

One former slave remembered the lunch, "baskets filled wid hot pone, baked taters, corn roasted in de shucks, onion, fried squash, an' b'iled pork. Sometimes dey brought buckets o' cold buttermilk . . . ." [41]

Henry Clay Bruce, a Missouri slave, wrote in retrospect,

"We were called up by the overseer by means of a horn, ate breakfast and were in the field by daylight, sometimes, before it was light enough to see the cotton balls, and kept steadily at work till noon, when dinner was brought to us on large trays and the order given by the overseer to eat. We sat down right there, and as soon as the last mouthful was swallowed the order was given to go to work. We were given good, wholesome food and plenty of it, only the time was so short in which to eat it." [42]

Virginia ex-slave Susan Jackson reported:

"At ten o'clock on work days dey would ring de bell an' dat was de sign fo' chillun to come fum de fiel'. Dey go back to de kitchen an' help A[u]nt Hannah fix de food. She would take de cakes out, an' we would den put 'em aside to warm on a big tray. De cook filled 'nother tray wid cabbage an' a bucket wid pot liquor. Den we take it all to de fiel', and de slaves lay down under a shade tree an' eat. Mos' times dey got half-hour, but nobody ain't gonna rush none." [43]

The communal cooking resulted in a better diet for the workers, for few slaves had adequate time or cooking facilities and equipment to produce ample, nourishing meals three times a day. — Even on the big land holdings, though, slaves were expected to prepare supper in their cabins over the coals of their mud-and-sticks fireplaces.

A description of the daily travail of one black woman in North Carolina is given by her son, James Curry:

"My mother's labor was very hard. She would go to the house in the morning, take her pail upon her head, and go away to the cow-pen, and milk fourteen cows. She then put on the bread for the family breakfast, and got the cream ready for churning, and set a little child to churn it, she having the care of from ten to fifteen children, whose mothers worked in the field. After clearing away the family breakfast, she got breakfast for the slaves; which consisted of warm corn bread and buttermilk, and was taken at twelve o'clock. In the meantime, she had beds to make, rooms to sweep, &c. Then she cooked the family dinner, which was simply plain meat, vegetables, and bread. Then the slaves' dinner was to be ready at from eight to nine o'clock in the evening. It consisted of corn bread, or potatoes, and the meat which remained of the master's dinner, or one herring apiece. At night she had the cows to milk again. There was little ceremony about the master's supper, unless there was company.

This was her work day by day. Then in the course of the week, she had washing and ironing to do for her master's family (who, however, were clothed very simply), and for her husband, seven children and herself.

"She would not get through to go to her log cabin until nine or ten o'clock at night. She would then be so tired, that she could scarcely stand, but she would find one boy with his knee out, and another with his elbow out, a patch wanting here, and a stitch there, and she would sit down by her lightwood fire, and sew and sleep alternately, often till the light began to streak in the east; and then lying down, she would catch a nap, and hasten to the toil of the day." [44]

One advantage of requiring slaves to prepare all their own meals was that slave cabin-centered food preparation lent a greater sense of cohesiveness to the individual family unit in which the mother prepared meals for her own husband and children. This responsibility was a burdensome one, though, for, as previously mentioned, the slaves had little in the way of utensils, etc. Under the system in which the workers provided their own meals, a majority of slaves were given a weekly ration of food. A peck of cornmeal per week for each adult and three or four pounds of salt pork or bacon (less for the children) was the typical ration, although a woman doctor from the North, Esther Hill Hawks, reported that on a particular plantation, heads of families received "a half *pint* of *homany* [hominy] and *three qtrs. pound* of *salt* pork, with a very small *allowance* for *each child*." [45] One slave remarked with dry humor, "[none of us was] ever likely to suffer from the gout, superinduced by excessive high living." [46] At times beef or mutton was given instead of pork, and some planters followed the advice of Dr. Jno. S. Wilson who suggested that "negroes should be liberally supplied with garden vegetables, and milk and [cane or sorghum] molasses should be given out occasionally at least. These afford an agreeable variety [supplementing the 'hog and hominy' diet] and serve as preventatives to scurvy and other diseases." [47]

Some slaveholders also added one or more of the following: Irish or sweet potatoes, rice, field peas, eggs and poultry, and perhaps even fruit, sugar and coffee to the slave rations. Slaves were, in some circumstances, permitted to raise a little vegetable garden of their own, and perhaps to keep chickens.[48] Yet many slaves were not well provided for. The corn issued at the corncrib and the bacon given out at the smokehouse on a Sunday morning might all be consumed before the week was over. (If this occurred other slaves often shared their food with the one whose portion was depleted, for the more strict owners or overseers allowed no more rations to be given until the normal distribution day.) Harsh masters were known to let their workers suffer lack of ample food even to the point of habitually issuing scanty rations as a form of "economy." One man reported, "Some of the plantations half-starved their [slaves] and 'lowanced out their eating till they wasn't fitting for work . . . ." [49] A former slave looked back, "I'll always hate her [her 'old mistress'] 'cos [because] she never give me 'nuff to eat, not till it 'spile [spoiled] when she done had 'nuff." [50]

Another person remarked,

"Dey never give you 'nough ter eat. I mos' nigh starved all de time. I useter sit by de side o' de fiahplace in de cabin an' po'ch [parch] co'n an' eat it." [51]

In general, though, records indicate that a majority had enough food, albeit seldom the better cuts of meat. A former Virginia slave, Bacchus White, remarked, "dey uster [they used to] give dem some of de shoulders if de middlings, jowls, and heads giv 'ert [give out; run out] . . . nuver had no hams." [52] According to Henry Clay Bruce:

"Some slave owners did not feed well causing their slaves to steal chickens, hogs and sheep from them or from other owners. Bacon and bread with an occasional meal of beef was the feed through the entire year; but our master gave us all we could eat, together with such vegetables as were raised on the farm. My mother was the cook for the families, white and black, and of course I fared well as to food." [53]

The diet was adequate calorie-wise (4000-5000 calories per day for the laborer),[54] but ofttimes nutritionally unbalanced and/or poorly prepared. One planter, in condemning the practice of requiring slaves to furnish their own meals, wrote,

"The cooking being done in a hurry, [due to hunger and lack of time] is badly done; being usually burnt [on the] outside while it is raw within; and consequently unhealthy. However abundant may be the supply of vegetables, the hands have no time to cook them, and consequently are badly fed, and have not the strength to do as much labor as they could otherwise perform with comfort." [55]

When slaves did cook their own meals, an iron pot and maybe a skillet were their cookware. Willis Cofer, a former slave, reported,

" . . . all our cookin' was done in de fireplace. Pots wuz hung on iron cranes to bile and big pones of light bread wuz cooked in [Dutch] ovens on de hearth. Dat light bread and de biscuits made out of shorts ["Shorts" are a by-product of milling, and may include the bran, germ, and other wheat particles after the white flour has been separated out.] wuz our Sunday bread, and dey sho' wuz good, wid our home-made butter. Us had good old corn bread for our evvyday bread, and dere ain't nothin' lak corn bread and buttermilk to make healthy [slaves] . . . de slaves got all de milk and butter dey needed [from the dairy house, and the meat ration from the smokehouse]." [56]

Recalled another black person,

"We didn't have stoves plentiful then: just ovens we set in the fireplace. Ah's toted many a armful of bark — good old hickory bark to cook with. We'd cook light bread — both flour and corn. The yeast fur this bread wuz made from hops. Coals of fire was put on top of the oven and under the bottom, too." [57]

Some slaves were allowed to supplement their diet by gunless hunting, fishing, and trapping.[58] One recalled,

"If we ever wanted fish, we could go fishing right on the place. We could hunt at night, but they wouldn't let us . . . have guns. We'd hunt with dogs." [59]

Henry Clay Bruce, a slave in Missouri, remembered,

"I was too young to be put to work, and there being on the farm four or five boys about my age, spent my time with them hunting and fishing. There was a creek near by in which we caught plenty of fish. We made lines of hemp grown on the farm and hooks of bent pins . . . But fish then were very plentiful and not as scary [skittish] as now . . . We often brought home as much as five pounds of fish in a day." [60]

Charlie Hudson, ex-slave from Georgia, stated,

> "Us ate good . . . Most times it was meat and bread wid turnip greens, lye hominy, milk, and butter. All our cookin' was done on open fireplaces. Oh! I was fond of 'possums, sprinkled with butter and pepper, and baked down 'till de gravy was good and brown." [61]

Opossums were normally treed at night and captured, then, as one slave instructed,

> " . . . put dem up and feed dem hoe-cake and [per]simmons ter git dem nice and fat; den my mammy would roast dem wid sweet potatoes round them. Dey wuz sho' good, all roasted nice and brown wid de sweet taters in de graby [gravy]." [62]

Wooden spoons were used; or oyster or mussel shells substituted. Georgia slave Benny Dillard recalled,

> "De wooden bowls what slave chillun et out of was made out of sweetgum trees. Us et wid mussel shells 'stid [instead] of spoons. Dem mussel shells was all right. Us could

use 'em to git [get] up plenty of bread and milk, or cornpone soaked wid peas and pot likker. Dey never let chillun have no meat 'til dey was big enough to wuk [work] in de fields. Us had biscuit once a week, dat was Sunday breakfast, and dem biscuits was cakebread to us." [63]

One slave mused,

"Potlicker and cornbread was fed to us chillun, out of big old wooden bowls. Two or three chillun et out of de same bowl. Grown folks had meat, greens, syrup, cornbread, 'taters and de lak [like]. 'Possums! I should say so. Dey cotch [caught] plenty of 'em and after dey was kilt Ma would scald 'em and rub 'em in hot ashes and dat clean't 'em just as pretty and white. . . . Dey used to go fishin' and rabbit huntin' too. Us jus' fetched in game galore den, for it was de style dem days. . . . Seemed lak [like] to me in dem days dat ash-roasted 'taters and groundpeas was de best something t'eat what anybody could want. 'Course dey had a gyarden, and it had somepin of jus' about evvything what us knowed anything 'bout in de way of gyarden sass growin' in it. All de cookin' was done in dem big old open fireplaces what was fixed up special for de pots and ovens. Ashcake was most as good as 'taters cooked in de ashes, but not quite." [64]

Another slave child memory:

"On all of his plantations dere was one old 'oman [woman] dat didn't have nothin' else to do but look [after] and cook for de [slave] chillun whilst dey mammies was at wuk in de fields. Aunt Viney tuk [took] keer of us. She had a big old horn what she blowed when it was time for us to eat, and us knowed better dan to git so fur off us couldn't hear dat horn, for Aunt Viney would sho' [sure] tear us up. Marster had done told her she better fix us plenty t'eat and give it to us on time. Dere was a great long trough what went plum 'cross de yard, and dat was whar us et. For dinner us had peas or some other sort of vegytables and cornbread. Aunt Viney crumbled up dat bread in de trough and poured de vegytables and pot-likker over it. Den she blowed de horn and chillun come a-runnin' from evvy which away. If us et it all up, she had to put more victuals in de trough. At nights, she crumbled de cornbread in de trough and poured buttermilk over it. Us never had nothin' but cornbread and buttermilk at night. Sometimes dat trough would be a sight, 'cause us never stopped to wash our hands, and 'fore us had been eatin' more dan a minute or two what was in de trough would look lak de red mud what had come off of our hands. Sometimes Aunt Viney would fuss at us and make us clean it out." [65]

Henry Clay Bruce reminisced,

"Such old women usually had to care for, and prepare the meals of all children under working age. They were furnished with plenty of good, wholesome food by the master, who took special care to see that it was properly cooked and served to them as often as they desired it.

> "On very large plantations there were many such old women, who spent the remainder of their lives caring for children of younger women. Masters took great pride in their gangs of young slaves, especially when they looked 'fat and sassy' . . . ." [66]

In explaining how to cook coush-coush (a sort of crumbled cornbread dish popular in Louisiana) overall advice for preparing food for the little ones is offered: "[It should be] good on de tongue en' easy on de stumick, da's how to cook fo' chilluns." [67]

Certain events were cause for celebration. Corn shuckings, hog-killing time, Christmas — these days were times of feasting. Luxuries such as white flour, sugar, eggs, coffee, a whole ham, etc.[68] might be given to members of the dark work force. Some recollected,

> " . . . [O]n Christmas Day . . . Marse Lordnorth [plantation 'boss' and cousin of the plantation owner, eventual Confederate Vice-President Alexander H. Stephens] and Marse Alec give us evvything you could

name to eat: Cake of all kinds, fresh meat, lightbread, turkeys, chickens, ducks, geese, and all kinds of wild game. Dere was allus plenty of pecans, apples, and dried peaches too at Christmas." [69]

"Chris'mas us went f'um house to house lookin' for locust and persimmon beer. [A Southern black tradition held that slaves could request gifts or treats from their masters on Christmas morning.] Chillun went to all de houses huntin' gingerbread. Ma used to roll it thin, cut it out wid a thimble, and give a dozen of dem little balls to each chile. Persimmon beer and gingerbread! What big times us did have at Chris'mas." [70]

"Them Christmas Days was something else! If I could call back one of them Christmas Days now, when I went up to the house and brung back my checkered apron full! . . . Great big round peppermint balls! Big bunches of raisins, we put aprons full on the bed and then went back to the house to get another apron full.

"We had good times at corn-shuckings too. Honey, I've seen my grandma, Icie, the cook, when they had corn-shuckings, the chickens she'd put in that big pot, hanging on one of them hooks in the kitchen fireplace. She put twelve chickens in that pot, grown hens, let them boil, put the dumplings in, call the darkies and give them a plate full. I just wish you could have been there and seen how my grandma made that gingerbread. They cooked that for corn-shuckings and used it for cake. It was better than what cake is now, and they gave them locust beer to drink with it." [71]

Much of the slave-cabin cooking, even if prepared hastily, was tasty. One-pot mixtures of vegetables with meat harkened back to African kitchen creations. Using cabbage leaves to wrap cornpones, sweet potatoes, and even chickens for roasting reflected the African manner of roasting foods in banana leaves.[72] A contemporary black cookbook writer offers a recipe for cabbage rolls and ham hocks simmered in tomato sauce. The cabbage leaves contain ground pork sausage, rice, seasonings, and eggs for binding together the mixture.[73] (Cabbage leaves are also used in French Canadian cookery. This practice can be traced back to the European use of grape and cabbage leaves, although blacks did migrate to Canada.)[74] Perhaps wild herbs were found by the enslaved, or cultivated herbs grown to enhance the flavor of a stew. By the time of the Civil War, black cooks were much in demand in the army, "as many were skilled in the arts of seasoning." [75]

A former slave in South Carolina, Lizzie Davis, told an interviewer, "Yes, child, de slavery people sho had de hand to cook." [76]

White writer Robert Q. Mallard remarked,

" . . . [F]or if there is any one thing for which the African female intellect has natural genius, it is for cooking . . . . French cooks are completely outdistanced in the production of wholesome, dainty and appetizing food." [77]

The creative black cook discovered ways to improve her (or his) cooking — honey from the forest could sweeten an herbal tea or kiss a hot biscuit. If no coffee was available a substitute could be made from sweet potatoes or cowpeas. Mashed cowpeas formed into a patty and fried in lard made a fine pea "cake" — a new dish for the United States, but a traditional African recipe.[78] Black cooks also gave cooked green vegetables flavor and "substance" by adding fat back or bacon.

The following major portion of this book, Chapter 4, contains recipes which celebrate this adaptability and ingenuity in creating things good "t' eat." Some of the recipes are historically authentic (as noted), others are the author's own commemorative adaptations, and several are typical modern interpretations of traditional favorites. May the reader enjoy preparing and tasting these examples of "Soul," whether on rice or not!

Chapter 4: "Our T' Eat"

Peanut Soup

Dr. George Washington Carver (1864? – 1943), the son of Missouri slaves, achieved international fame because of his agriculture research. He concentrated on Southern crops such as peanuts, sweet potatoes, and pecans. From the peanut Dr. Carver made more than 300 products, including soap, ink, dyes, pickles, and kinds of milk, butter, cheese, and "instant" coffee.

Peanut soup is now a Dixie classic.

* * *

$1/2$ c. onion, finely chopped

2 tbsp. vegetable oil

$3/4$ c. creamy peanut butter

3 c. chicken broth

Salt and pepper to taste

Cook onion in oil until soft and golden brown. Blend in peanut butter. Add chicken broth, stirring constantly until mixture is smooth. Bring to boil, then lower heat, and simmer 10 minutes. Makes 4 to 5 servings.

African Main Dish Peanut Butter Sauce

The following recipe puts a sample of African-style eating on the American table.

* * *

2 tbsp. vegetable oil

$1/2$ c. onion, chopped

2 cloves garlic, minced

$1/2$ c. peanut butter

$1/2$ c. water

2 tbsp. tomato paste *or* 1 or 2 fresh chopped tomatoes

2 to 3 c. water, vegetable cooking water, *or* stock

Salt, pepper, hot peppers to taste

1 tbsp. lemon juice (optional)

Chopped, cooked chicken, fish, *or* beef (optional)

Chunks of cooked pumpkin *or* sweet potato (optional)

Sliced squash *or* okra (optional)

1 to 2 c. chopped greens (optional)

Heat the oil in a large pot. Add the onion and garlic and sauté until the onion is tender. Meanwhile make a paste of the $1/2$ c. peanut butter and the $1/2$ c. water. Blend this and the tomato paste into the cooked onion/garlic mixture. Slowly add 2 or 3 cups water or other liquid to achieve the thickness of sauce you like, stirring and cooking all the while. Season to taste, and, if desired, add one or more of the optional ingredients, heating or cooking as need be. Serve over rice or other starch.

Note: You can brown uncooked chicken, beef, lamb, etc. along with the onion and garlic, and then cook the sauce at least an hour until the meat is done.

Thoughts: This is a dish for experimentation. Different herbs and seasonings can be used, amounts varied, etc. Have fun!

New Orleans Rice

A foodwriter named Jane Eddington visited the French Market and other locations in New Orleans in 1912 and, from a black lady, learned these rice-cooking instructions:

* * *

"Put some rice to it is the direction, seemingly, for at least half or even more of the stews and soups and related dishes made in New Orleans. But in many cases the meat seems to be put to the rice — there is so much more rice than meat.

"A dark-hued cook, in her delightfully mellow voice, explained to me how she prepared her rice for meat dishes. She put some rice into boiling water — after washing it — and let it boil twenty minutes. She poured this out into a colander, rinsed it in cold water, and then set it back in the colander over boiling water to steam done. Cooked in this way 'each grain was to itself.' " [79]

Gravy for Rice

Mrs. V.D. Covington, who was visiting Brunson's Station in South Carolina in 1880, wrote:

* * *

"Those who can [hire] colored cooks have their kitchen separate from the dwelling house, and abjure stoves and modern conveniences . . . because . . . [the cooks] prefer to cook in the old-fashioned fire place. . . . Entering, you observe smoky rafters and an immense black, yawning fire place, in which, or near it, are numerous cooking vessels of various sizes . . . . Smuttiness is generated in southern kitchens by the burning of lightwood knots, which Aunt Dinah prefers to any other kind of wood.

" . . . very delicious are the comestibles she turns out of those same pots. There are sweet potatoes, large, sugary, candied fellows, (I am writing this before day[break] and stopped to eat a baked one to be sure of realizing just how nice it was).

"Then there is rice, the colored [cook] never makes a failure in cooking it, if it's a quart or a peck she will be sure to have it white, firm-grained, every kernel distinct, and yet 'done to a turn.'

"We want gravy to eat with it, and that is made as follows: After taking out the meat that has been baked or fried, the vessel is returned to the fire and a cup of sweet milk, to which has been added a little salt, black pepper and flour, is poured into it and stirred for four or five minutes." [80]

Deep South Brown Rice

This recipe was said to have been "cooked at Bay Brook, by Mam Jinks, for visitors from the 'North.' "

* * *

"Brown rice is delicious and is richer in minerals than polished rice but is not often used.

"One cup of [brown] rice, one teaspoon of salt and four cups of water are the proportions. Wash the rice well, then boil over flame in a large quantity of water for ten minutes. When the water has boiled away place in the inner part of the double boiler and cook forty-five minutes or longer. Especially good when served with a whole roasted pig." [81]

Soul on Rice Chicken

Also using brown rice, this modern recipe is easy and savory.

* * *

2 c. water

1 tbsp. chicken bouillon granules (*or* use 2 c. chicken broth instead of water and bouillon)

1 c. onion, chopped

1 lg. clove garlic (1 tsp. minced)

1 c. tomatoes (canned *or* fresh), chopped

1/2 tsp. poultry seasoning

1/4 tsp. salt

1/8 tsp. pepper

4 to 5 pieces of chicken

1 tbsp. spicy brown mustard

1 (10-oz.) pkg. frozen chopped greens

1 1/3 c. uncooked brown rice

Stew together until the chicken is tender.

Congo Fish/American Version

1 tbsp. butter

1 tbsp. peanut oil

1 c. onion, chopped

1/2 c. green pepper, chopped

1/4 tsp. black pepper

2 c. water

1 lb. greens (collards, kale, spinach, etc.)

1 lb. frozen fish fillets, slightly thawed

Cayenne pepper and salt to taste

Sauté the onion and green pepper in the fat. When soft, add water, greens, and fish cut into chunks. Cover, cooking until tender. (Add more water if necessary.) Season to taste. Serve over *fufu* or rice.

George Washington Carver's Mock Chicken

"Blanch and grind a sufficient number of peanuts until they are quite oily; stir in one well-beaten egg; if too thin, thicken with rolled bread crumbs or cracker dust; stir in [a] little salt. Boil some sweet potatoes until done; peel and cut in thin slices; spread generously with the peanut mixture; dip in white of egg; fry to a chicken brown; serve hot." [82]

One-time slave Cornelius Garner stated, "A good eatin' meal consist o' fish or fried meat, 'lasses an' bread." [83]

Santee Catfish Stew

Catfish have long been a favorite fish among the black community.

* * *

6 medium-sized freshwater fish *or* catfish

2 (10¾ oz.) cans condensed tomato soup

½ lb. onions

1 sm. bottle tomato catsup

Few drops Worcestershire sauce

¼ lb. salt pork, diced

½ stick (¼ c.) butter

1 tsp. black pepper

Dash cayenne

Salt to taste

    Combine soup and catsup and boil slowly. Fry salt pork and sauté onions until tender. Add with all other ingredients, except fish, plus 1 c. water if too thick. Boil 5 minutes. Drop in fish which have been cut into small pieces and cook about 5 more minutes. Serve over rice or with hush puppies. Serves 6.[84]

Oyster Soup

An African-American newspaper published the following because, they stated, "oyster soup is always immensely popular":

* * *

"Take one quart of oysters, and separate them from the liquor, wash them thoroughly in a pint of water, strain the liquor, add one pint of milk, some mace, nutmeg and pepper, three crackers pounded fine; add one fourth pound of butter to the liquor, boil all together about five minutes, and take it off the fire. When about to serve up the soup, put in the oysters and let it all boil one minute. The soup will then be ready for the table. For each quart of oysters a pint of milk must be added, and other ingredients in proportion to the quantity required." [85]

Panned Oysters

This recipe was attributed to an African-American cook in the 1880s:

* * *

"Drain the oysters, then wash and wipe them dry. In a shallow dripping pan, melt a large lump of butter, without allowing it to brown. Throw in the oysters and shake and stir them constantly until they are sufficiently cooked, then lay them on slices of toast arranged in a dish beforehand. It is better to do a few at a time, and send them to the table in relays, so that the toast may not become sodden." [86]

Fried Oysters

Drain fresh oysters in a colander, and then roll each oyster in cornmeal seasoned with salt and pepper. Fry the oysters in deep hot fat, cooking only a few at a time, until golden brown. Drain on paper towels.

Fried Frog Legs

Cut legs off the frog, skin them, and soak them overnight in salted water under refrigeration. Fry just as you would fry chicken. (Don't be surprised when the legs start jumping in the skillet.)

Harlem Gumbo (Stewed Mackerel)

This easy, economical entrée has a flavor reminiscent of gumbo.

* * *

1½ c. canned tomatoes, cut up (include some of the tomato liquid)

½ c. onion, chopped

½ c. green pepper, chopped

Salt, pepper, and crushed red pepper to taste

1 can mackerel, undrained

Cooked rice

Put the tomatoes, onion, green pepper, and seasonings in a pot. Cook, covered, for about 15 minutes, stirring ever so often. Add the mackerel, breaking up slightly. Heat. Serve the rice and Harlem Gumbo in two separate bowls. Let diner(s) put a mound of rice on his or her plate and then ladle on the stewed fish.

Chicken Gumbo

1 small stewing chicken

2 tbsp. all-purpose flour

3 tbsp. butter, melted

1 onion, chopped

4 c. okra, sliced and chopped

2 c. tomato pulp

Few sprigs parsley, chopped

4 c. water

Salt and pepper to taste

    After chicken is cleaned and dressed, cut it into serving portions. Dredge lightly with the flour and sauté in the butter, along with the chopped onion. When the chicken is nicely browned, add the okra, tomatoes, parsley, and water. Season to taste with salt and pepper. Cook very slowly until the chicken is tender and the okra well-cooked — about 2½ hours. Add water as required during the slow cooking process. If a thin soup is preferred, the quantity of water may be increased.[87]

African-Style Chicken Stew

(A first cousin to African Main Dish Peanut Butter Sauce, p. 41.)

* * *

2 tbsp. vegetable oil

1 c. onion, chopped

2 cloves garlic, minced

3 tbsp. all-purpose flour

$1/4$ tsp. salt

Dash of pepper

2 c. canned, chopped, undrained tomatoes

1 c. chicken broth

$1/4$ tsp. crushed red pepper

$1/2$ c. peanut butter

2 c. cooked, chopped chicken

Cooked rice

Sauté the onion and garlic in the oil. When the onion is translucent, stir in the flour. Stir and cook a few minutes, and then add salt, pepper, tomatoes, and chicken broth. Simmer together for around 20 minutes. Add crushed red pepper and peanut butter, and stir well. Gently stir in chicken and heat. Serve over rice or other starch base.

The two following recipes are credited to " 'Uncle John,' Chef of Mr. LeGaree, of South Carolina" in Célestine Eustis' 1903 *Cooking in Old Créole Days*.

Terrapin Stew

"Boil your terrapin soft. Put in a small piece of bacon, one or two onions, pepper and butter. Chop fine two or three hard boiled eggs. Put all together. Add a little wine." [88]

Partridge à la "Uncle John"

"Take six or eight partridges, or small quails, brown them in a small pan with lard and a light sprinkling of flour. Add three tablespoons of raw tomatoes, half a cupful of meat juice, onion, salt and pepper. Let them simmer an hour, covered. Baste them from time to time with the gravy. Serve with hot rice." [89]

Creole Jambalaya

Black chefs made Louisiana Creole cuisine world famous with imaginative combinations like the one below. Incidentally, it is said that "the traditional cooking of New Orleans is perhaps the closest to that of the West African coast that you can find in the United States." [90]

* * *

1 tbsp. fat *or* oil

2 lg. onions, chopped

1 clove garlic, minced

3/4 c. green pepper, chopped

1 sprig parsley, chopped

1 lb. cooked ham, cubed

2 tbsp. all-purpose flour

2 1/2 c. water

5 c. tomatoes, diced

2 c. uncooked white rice

1 bay leaf

Salt and pepper

3 c. shrimp

Put the fat in a large pot. Add the next five ingredients and sauté a few minutes. Stir in the flour, and cook, stirring constantly for five minutes. Add the rest of the ingredients, and bring to a boil, stir, cover, reduce heat and simmer for 30 minutes. Remove bay leaf before serving. Serves 12.

Carolina Pigs' Feet

"First clean them well by dipping them in scalding water, and scraping off the hairs and hoofs, after which put them into weak salt and water for a day. They are then ready to boil for souse.

"If, however, you wish to keep them for frying, or stewing, they may be preserved in this weak salt and water for three or four weeks. If the weather is warm, the salt and water may require [changing]. They must be soaked in fresh water all night, before boiling them. Boil them in cold water until tender.

"[If you wish] to stew pigs' feet . . . Boil four feet, take out the bones, and put them in a vessel with a little vinegar and water, a lump of butter the size of a goose egg, and some salt and pepper, and stew for half an hour, and serve on a hot dish. Or they are nice dressed as terrapins.

"[If you wish] to fry pigs' feet . . . split them in halves lengthwise, dip them in batter, and fry in hot lard. They must previously have been soaked several hours in vinegar.

"You can [also] fry them in vinegar and water without lard, and they will be very nice." [91]

Boiled Pigs' Feet

6 to 8 pigs' feet

2 onions, sliced

4 ribs of celery (optional)

Salt and pepper

Put a piece of aluminum foil in the bottom of a large pot. (This keeps the feet from sticking to the bottom.) Place pigs' feet in the pot. Cover with water, bring to a boil, and simmer, covered, about an hour. Add onion and celery (if liked), salt and pepper, and more water as needed to maintain at least a depth of one inch. Keep cooking, covered, until the meat is tender and almost falling off the bone. This will probably take two additional hours.

Fried Chitterlings

You eat every part of the pig but the oink. . . .

* * *

1 pkg. frozen chitterlings

1 egg, beaten

1 c. bread *or* cracker crumbs, fine

Deep fat

1 tsp. whole cloves

1 sm. hot pepper, chopped

1 qt. boiling, salted water

Thaw "chitlins" in cold water. Drain and clean well. Cover with boiling salted water to which 1 tsp. whole cloves and pepper have been added. Cook until tender. Drain. Cut into small pieces, dip into beaten egg, and then roll in crumbs. Fry in deep fat until golden.[92]

Field Peas

This African staple became a Southern palate necessity. The first recorded recipe for preparing field peas (also known as cowpeas, cornfield peas, or black-eyed peas or beans) is found in Mary Randolph's *The Virginia Housewife* cookbook (from an edition published in the 1820s).

* * *

"There are many varieties of these peas; the smaller kind are the most delicate. Have them young and newly gathered, shell and boil them tender; pour them in a colander to drain; put some lard in a frying-pan; when it boils, mash the peas, and fry them in a cake of a light brown; put it in the dish with the crust uppermost — garnish with thin bits of fried bacon. They are very nice when fried whole, so that each pea is distinct from the other; but they must be boiled less, and fried with great care. Plain boiling is a very common way of dressing them." [93]

"Alabama Baked Cow Peas (Delicious)"

"Soak one pint of peas in cold water over night or until the hulls rub off easily, free them from the skins by rubbing them between the hands; continue washing in cold water until all the skins are removed; put in vessel to cook (porcelain or granite stew-pan preferable), with just enough water to cover them . . . put in small piece of fat pork, boil the peas until about half done, pour into baking dish, season to taste with butter, pepper and salt, put tablespoonful of sugar to every quart of peas; put in oven, cook slowly until well done and brown; serve hot or cold." [94]

"Ochra [Okra] and Tomatos [Tomatoes]"

This is another 1820s African-influenced cookbook entry.

* * *

"Take an equal quantity of each, let the ochra be young, slice it, and skin the tomatoes; put them into a pan without water, add a lump of butter, an onion chopped fine, some pepper and salt, and stew them one hour." [95]

Tuskegee Institute Tomato and Okra Soup

"Use —

1½ pints of tomatoes pared and cut fine,

2 quarts water,

1 pint sliced okra,

3 tablespoons rice,

3 tablespoons (or 1 large) minced onion [according to cook's discretion],

1 green pepper chopped fine (seeds removed),

Salt to taste [Confusingly, there are two versions of this recipe in the same pamphlet; in one 3 teaspoons of salt were called for, in the other 3 tablespoons were suggested! Both amounts are more than modern taste would consider palatable.]

¼ teaspoon black pepper,

3 tablespoons green corn.

"Put all the ingredients into the soup pot, and cook gently for two hours; then add two tablespoons butter or sweet drippings, and serve. The bones from roast meat or broiled meat adds to its flavor." [96]

Fried Okra

Okra

Salt

Flour

Cornmeal

Shortening *or* bacon grease

Wash the okra and cut off the ends. Then slice the okra into $1/4$ - inch pieces. Meanwhile mix equal parts flour and cornmeal in a paper bag. (Some folks prefer a much greater ratio of cornmeal to flour — suit yourself.) Add salt and pepper. Put the okra, a little at a time, into the bag, and shake it around to coat it. When all of the okra is coated, fry it in ½ inches fat in a skillet. Turn the okra over to lightly brown all surfaces. Serve good and hot.

Note: Some cooks prepare fried okra by boiling the pods first, cooking until tender. Then season with salt and pepper, dip in beaten egg, roll in cornmeal and fry in deep fat.

Foodways

Favorite "soul foods" include cornbreads, biscuits, fried chicken and fish, turtle stew and soup, barbecue, "pig parts," dressing (as for turkey), poke salad, potato salad, berry cobbler ("dubie"), and indescribably good cakes. (Jeannette Wright Shamwell remembered her mother baking "pies, plain cake, marble cake, coconut cake, chocolate cake . . . Lady Baltimore cake" at Christmastime.[97]) Many of these foods have become such standard American fare that any inclusive cookbook gives such recipes. Written recipes for other black foods are a little less easy to find.

"How to Cook Egg-Plant."

"I take a large-sized egg-plant, leave the stem and skin on, and boil it in a porcelain kettle until very soft, just so you can get it out with the aid of a fork and spoon. Then take all the skin off, mash it very fine in a bowl (not tin or earthen). Add a teaspoonful of salt, plenty of pepper, a large iron spoonful of flour (when it is cold), a half-teacupful of milk or cream, and three eggs. This forms a nice batter. Now have some butter and lard brown-hot, and drop the batter in with a spoon, as you would fritters, and brown them nicely each side." [98]

New Potatoes with Salt Pork

3 qts. *or* more small new potatoes, not peeled

Water to cover

Plenty of salt

¾ lb. streak-of-lean salt pork, chopped

Handful of spring onions with tops, chopped

Black pepper

    Cook the potatoes in the salted water. Meanwhile fry the salt pork 'til crisp. Remove the pork from the skillet, leaving the grease in the pan. Add the onions to the grease and cook until tender. Remove the onions from the skillet. Combine the cooked potatoes, the crispy salt pork, and the onions in a large bowl. Season with pepper, and serve with pride.

Collard Greens with Ham Hocks

Put two ham hocks in a large pot. Cover with water, bring to a boil, and then simmer for 1 to 2 hours or until the meat is fork tender. (Add more water as needed.) Remove ham hocks from pot; cut skin and meat off, and discard the bones. Chop the skin and meat into small pieces and return to the pot. (Some people discard the skin.)

Take 2 to 3 lbs. collard greens. Remove the lower stems and discard. Wash the remaining leaves. Chop. Put the collards into the pot of meat and cooking liquid. Season with salt, pepper, and a teaspoon of sugar. Bring to a boil, then cover and reduce heat. Simmer for about two hours. Cook down to a "low gravy."

Note: Ham hock seasoning (the hocks and their cooking liquid as described above) can also be used as a medium in which to cook black-eyed peas, beans, cabbage, etc.

Bacchus White remembered,

"Dey uster to 'ave a big garden. I 'spose hit was a acre and a half, uster to ra'se all kinds of vegetables. [We] never did eat 'pargus and green peas 'till after de war, never liked dem . . . [Our mistress] nuver 'llowed cab'age on [her] table, she did'nt like de smell of dem." [99]

Greens Another Way

2 to 2½ lbs. fresh greens (mustard, turnip, collards, etc.) — Known as a "mess o' greens," "mess" meaning a quantity of greens, other vegetables, or meat sufficient to serve a given number of people.

¼ lb. salt pork, diced

½ c. boiling water

Salt

Wash the greens thoroughly. Cook pork in the boiling water about 10 minutes; then add the greens, a few at a time. Cover the pot and simmer until the greens are tender.

Poke Salad (or "Sallet")

Pick young and tender poke sprouts. These sprouts should be only 6 to 8 inches tall. Do not cut the stalks below the surface of the ground. Do not eat poke after the plant has bloomed and has berries. Remove the leaves from the stems. Wash. Put in a pot and parboil for 5 minutes. Drain off the water. Put the salad into a skillet with bacon drippings and $1/2$ c. chopped onion (if enjoyed). Simmer the greens until the onions are soft. Add four eggs, and scramble gently. Season to taste with salt and pepper. — "Extry" good served with cornbread.

Hopping John

Black-eye or black-eyed peas (or Congris, cowpeas, Crowder peas, field peas, red peas, whip-or-will peas, black-betty — the nomenclature for similar legumes or pulse is not agreed upon even among experts) and rice are the two primary ingredients in this African-American dish.[100]

Otherwise, the dish represents authentic African cuisine. This particular basic dish was quickly adopted by the planters for use on their elegant tables, despite the fact that in the minds of the white aristocracy, earthy beans and rice was definitely a food of the "lower class." [101]

* * *

1 lb. dried black-eyed peas (rinsed and drained)

3 pt. cold water

½ lb. sliced salt pork *or* bacon

1 tsp. Tabasco sauce

2 tbsp. bacon fat *or* lard

2 medium onions, chopped

1 c. uncooked long-grain rice

1½ c. boiling water

Cover the peas with cold water in a large kettle. Soak overnight. (The modern method for cooking dried peas requires bringing them to a boil, simmering them for two minutes, and letting them stand for an hour.) Add salt pork, Tabasco, and salt. Cover and cook over low heat about 30 minutes. Meanwhile, cook onions in bacon fat until yellow and add to peas with rice and boiling water. Cook until rice is tender and water is absorbed, about 20 to 25 minutes, stirring occasionally. Yield: About eight servings.[102]

Hoe Cake

"Hoecake was meal mixed with water in a thick batter. Got its name from some of 'em slappin' it on a hoe an' holdin' it in de fire place tell [until] its cooked. Mother ain' done that. She used to cook hoecakes in a big iron pan, two or three at time. Simple fare, it was, but they was always plenty of it." [103]

* * *

"Moisten salted corn meal with scalding water or milk. Allow it to stand for an hour. Put two or three teaspoons of this on hot greased griddle. Smooth it out to make cakes one-half inch thick and let it cook. When one side is done turn over and brown the other. Serve very hot for breakfast. This dish goes well with sausage." [104]

Another Way to Make Hoecakes

"Take a large cupful of corn meal, sift it in a bowl, one pinch of salt, mix it with a little boiling water. Let it get cold. Make some small round cakes, pinch them on top. Put in a pan to bake in the oven." [105]

Aunt Milly's Mush Muffins

"Aunt Milly" was described as "a genius" cook who was "mistress of her art." She lived in Tennessee in the 1890s. A white writer endeavored to write down Milly's recipe for mush muffins, which was rather complicated. Here is the ingredient list first:

* * *

1 teacupful of meal (the white Southern meal)

1 piece of lard the size of a walnut

1 pinch of salt, say a quarter of a teaspoonful

3 cups of boiling water

"Aunt Milly . . . moves leisurely across to the stove, and stirs the fire, a roaring one already, for you have to have a hot oven for mush muffins.

"The kettle is throwing out a cloud of steam, and she takes the shallow pan in which she makes our dainty — the meal is already in there, an ordinary tea-cupful, with a piece of lard the size of a walnut. She pours the boiling water, a cupful, on the meal, stirring with a most careless hand, apparently, until the mixture is tolerably smooth, then pushes the pan aside and devotes her attention to something else, saying she 'don't see why folks think mush muffins hard to make. She don't have no trouble.' . . .

"Now Aunt Milly pours on the rest of the water, sets the pan on the fire, stirring hard, until it is quite transparent looking — that takes two minutes; then she places it on the table for ten minutes, when it is cool enough to add the egg. After stirring well, she proceeds to drop a spoonful of the batter into the smoking hot muffin rings, and the mush muffins are ready for the oven, where they will stay nearly a half hour.

"Eaten with sweet golden butter just from the spring, they seem to make you more hungry with each crisp mouthful. And with chicken fried a golden brown, with delicious broiled ham, beaten biscuit and Aunt Milly's good coffee, you do not envy a king. And then her waffles! Her crackers and egg-bread, to say nothing of dessert . . . ." [106]

Alabama Fare

In the 1920s, Clement Wood wrote down a typical menu of the food that was eaten at "Negro field cabins and the mountain and mill-town white houses" and a second menu of the foods eaten by "the more prosperous white and Negro families."

The poorer menu included:

Sow-belly (fat white pork)

(For a special occasion, fried chicken or 'possum an' 'taters might be substituted for the pork.)

Turnip greens and pot liquor (the latter the water in which the greens are cooked)

String beans, snap beans, boiled onions, or some other cooked vegetable in season

Corn pone (baked of cornmeal, salt and water)

Coffee with "long sweetening" — or molasses

No dessert

The more prosperous menu featured:

Fried young chicken

Beaten biscuits and corn pone

(An eccentric addition would be persimmon bread or sweet potato bread)

Stewed okra

Turnip greens

Mashed yams with pecans and cream

Rice

Coffee with cream

Fig Preserves

Crab-apple Jelly

Quince Preserves

Garden Tomatoes with sugar and vinegar

Ambrosia (equal parts of orange, pineapple and coconut, served in orange baskets) or Syllabub (whipped cream sweetened and flavored with vanilla)

Lady Baltimore Cake (a homelier dessert would be molasses pie, with molasses biscuit for the children)

If alcohol was served, scuppernong wine, muscadine wine, or a mint julep before the meal were possibilities.[107]

"Rice with Fruit"

"Parboil rice in water, then add milk, sugar, a little lemon peel or extract, and nutmeg, if liked a little butter, and the yolks of three eggs beaten up; cook until done; then place layer of stewed fruit of any kind on a dish, then a layer of rice over it; next another layer of fruit and then a layer of rice, and so on. It may be served hot or cold." [108]

Poor Man's French Toast

"Put some New Orleans molasses in a frying-pan, and let it boil until it thickens and is about half an inch deep in the pan. Slice some bread, removing the crust, and cut into squares or triangles. Butter them and lay them in the boiling molasses until they become crisp. Pile on a platter, hot." [109]

Yummy Yams [Sweet Potatoes]

Yams and sweet potatoes are botanically different. Nevertheless, the names are often used interchangeably.

* * *

4 large yams, pared, boiled, and sliced

$1/4$ c. butter *or* margarine, cut into pieces

$1/2$ c. brown sugar, packed

$1/2$ tsp. cinnamon

$1/2$ tsp. nutmeg

Place the tubers in a baking dish. Add remaining ingredients. Bake at 350° F. 'til bubbly. At this point, one may top with miniature marshmallows, and heat until the marshmallows are toasted.

Sweet-Potato Pudding, Circa 1830

"Boil one pound of sweet potatoes very tender, rub them while hot through a colander; add six eggs well beaten, three quarters of a pound of powdered sugar, three quarters of butter, and some grated nutmeg and lemon peel, with a glass of brandy; put a paste in the dish, and when the pudding is done, sprinkle the top with sugar, and cover it with bits of citron. Irish potato pudding is made in the same manner, but is not so good." [110]

Modern Sweet Potato Pudding

2 to 2½ lbs. fresh sweet potatoes

1 egg (beaten thoroughly)

½ c. Half-and-Half

1/8 tsp. vanilla extract

4 tbsp. butter

1/4 c. brown sugar

1/4 tsp. cinnamon

1 dash salt

To prepare the pudding: Wash the sweet potatoes thoroughly. Cut the larger potatoes in half and boil in the jackets until well cooked. Let the potatoes cool, peel them, and mash until quite smooth. Preheat oven to 350° F. Mix the cream and the vanilla with the beaten egg. Set aside. Melt the butter, add the brown sugar, and melt the sugar also. Add the cinnamon and the salt. Set this mixture aside. Combine the egg mixture with the sweet potatoes and mix thoroughly. Add the butter mixture and mix well. Put the mixture in a buttered casserole and bake for 35 to 40 minutes. Serves six to eight.[111]

Hasty Sweet Potato Pie

1 (16-oz.) can sweet potatoes, drained and mashed

1 (14-oz.) can sweetened condensed milk

2 eggs

1 tsp. vanilla

$1/2$ tsp. nutmeg

1 unbaked 9-inch pie shell

Using an electric mixer, blend together the first five ingredients; then pour into the pastry shell. Bake at 425° F. for 15 minutes. Reduce heat to 350° F. and bake about 30 minutes more, or until a knife inserted near the center comes out clean.

Black cooks learned to incorporate some of their staple foods into desserts. Sweet potatoes, as demonstrated, were (and are) used in puddings, pies, bread, and even pound cake. Cooked and mashed dried beans found their way into candies, cakes, and pies.

Pinto Bean Cake

1 c. sugar

1 stick ($1/2$ c.) butter *or* margarine

2 tsp. vanilla

2 eggs

2 c. cooked unseasoned pinto beans, mashed

1 c. all-purpose flour

1 tsp. baking soda

$1/2$ tsp. salt

1 tsp. cinnamon

1 tsp. allspice *or* $1/2$ tsp. cloves

$1/2$ c. nuts, chopped

1 c. raisins

2 c. finely-chopped peeled apples

Cream sugar and butter or margarine; add vanilla and eggs. Mix in well-mashed beans; stir in dry ingredients, then add nuts, raisins, and apples. Bake in a greased and floured tube pan for one hour at 325° F.

Sweet and Spicy Pork Cake

1 lb. fat salt pork

1 lb. raisins

2 c. sugar

1 c. molasses

2 eggs

5 c. all-purpose flour (approximately)

2 tsp. cinnamon

1 tsp. cloves

1 tsp. mace

1 tsp. baking soda

Put pork and raisins through food chopper together. Pour over them 1 pt.

boiling water; cool. Add eggs, sugar and molasses (well beaten). Sift together flour, spices, and baking soda. Stir into other ingredients. Beat thoroughly. Bake in 2 loaf tins lined with greased paper for about an hour in a slow oven (275° to 300° F.), or until a toothpick inserted in the center of the loaf comes out un-sticky.

Pork Fruit Cake

"One pound fat salt pork, one-half pint boiling water, two pounds raisins, [one] cup of sugar, one cup molasses, one teaspoon soda, one ounce cloves, two ounces cinnamon, one nutmeg [grated], and six cups flour. Grind the pork fine and pour the boiling water over it. Cook the raisins and roll in the same flour you use for the cake. The longer this stands the better." [112]

Molasses Cake

"A cupful of sugar and a cupful of butter stirred to a cream, then a cupful of molasses and a cupful of milk with a teaspoonful of baking powder, five eggs beaten very light; then stir in the other ingredients alternately with a cupful of flour. Stir the batter well and bake it quickly." [113]

Short'nin' Bread

1 lb. butter

1 c. light brown sugar

4 c. all-purpose flour

Cream together the butter and brown sugar. Gradually add the flour until it is all well-mixed. Place on floured surface and pat to one-half inch thickness. Cut into desired shapes and bake in moderate oven (325°-350° F.) for 20 to 25 minutes.[114]

Philadelphia Groundnut Cakes

" . . . there was a time — not so very long ago, either — when every Philadelphia child was familiar with the peanut or groundnut cakes, as they were called. They were sold on the corners of streets by old colored women wearing gorgeous-hued Madras turbans and spotless aprons. They sat on low stools and had their tempting wares neatly arranged on linen-covered trays. Likely the tubaned heads are laid low by this time, for we rarely see [the women] and never see the groundnut cakes. It was a savant who said that old recollections were revived more vividly through the taste than any other of the senses. For the benefit, then, of those who may care to recall the days when they bought ground nut cakes from their picturesque vendors, I append the original recipe for Philadelphia groundnut cakes.

"Boil two pounds of light-brown sugar in a preserving-kettle, with just enough water to thoroughly wet it, and when this sirup begins to boil throw in the white of an egg to clear it. Let it boil until a few drops of the sirup put into cold water become brittle; it is then sufficiently done, and must be taken from the fire and strained. Have ready a quarter of a peck of groundnuts, roasted in the shell and then shelled and hulled. Mix the nuts thoroughly through the sirup while it is yet hot. Dampen with a brush a pasteboard or marble slab, free from all grease, and drop the hot mixture upon it in little lumps, which must be flattened with a spoon into thin cakes the size of a tumbler-top. When cold take them off of the board with a knife." [115]

Peanut Candy

4 c. molasses

1 c. brown sugar

1 stick ($1/2$ c.) butter

4 c. roasted peanuts

    Simmer together the first three ingredients for half an hour. Add the peanuts and cook 15 minutes. Pour into a greased shallow pan. When hard break into pieces.

Peanut Butter Cookies

$2 1/2$ c. all-purpose flour

$1/2$ tsp. salt

$1/2$ tsp. baking soda

1 c. fat (margarine, butter, *or* shortening)

1 c. smooth or crunchy peanut butter

1 c. white sugar

1 c. brown sugar, packed

2 eggs

Mix flour, salt, and baking soda. Set aside. Mix fat and peanut butter. Add both kinds of sugar. Mix well. Add eggs and beat well. Stir flour mixture into peanut butter mixture. Drop dough from a teaspoon onto a baking sheet. Flatten with a fork, making a crisscross pattern. Bake at 375° F. (moderate oven) 10 to 15 minutes until lightly browned. Makes 4 to 5 dozen cookies. Note: For a nice surprise, add sesame seeds.[116]

Peach Pie

This was called "the best fruit pie that can be made" in the *Freedom's Journal* of 1828:

* * *

"Place your paste [crust] in a *deep plate* as for other pies, then, having wiped your peaches with a cloth, put them in *whole*, and spread upon them sugar sufficient to sweeten them *well*, then cover close with paste and bake till the fruit is sufficiently cooked. The stones [pits] of the peaches are sufficient without any other seasoning, and are better than any other. If the fruit is good, there will be so much of the juice on opening that it will be necessary to serve with a spoon." [117]

Note: Warn eaters about the pits!

Delicious Grape Pie

One quart canned grapes, three cups sugar, three teaspoons corn starch, previously mixed with juice of grapes, butter [the] size of [an] egg, melt the butter, bake with two crusts. Cherries can be used the same way. This makes three pies. If fresh cherries or grapes are used, they should be cooled on ice before mixing [with] the corn starch, sugar, butter.[118]

Note: It is best to use seedless grapes in this recipe.

Notes

[1] Nzingha Dalila, Harriet Beecher Stowe House, Cincinnati, Ohio, telephone conversation with author, August 13, 1991.

[2] Stacy Gibbons Moore, "Established and Well Cultivated: Afro-American Foodways in Early Virginia," *Virginia Cavalcade*, Virginia State Library and Archives, Richmond, Virginia, Autumn 1989, p. 75.

[3] Tadeusz Lewicki, *West African Food in the Middle Ages*, Cambridge University Press, New York, 1974, p. 79.

[4] Jessica B. Harris, *Iron Pots and Wooden Spoons*, Atheneum, New York, 1989, p. *xiii*.

[5] Helen Mendes, *The African Heritage Cookbook*, The Macmillan Company, New York, p. 36.

[6] Tami Hultman, editor, *The African News Cookbook: African Cooking for Western Kitchens*, African News Service, Inc., Viking, New York, 1985, p. *ix*.

[7] Betty Fussell, *I Hear America Cooking*, Elisabeth Sifton Books, Viking, New York, 1986, p. 147.

[8] Lewicki, p. 52.

[9] Donald Gilbert Coursey, *Yams*, Longmans, London, 1967, p. 199.

[10] *Ibid.*, p. 202.

[11] Mendes, p. 37.

[12] Lewicki, p. 20.

[13] Harris, p. 96.

[14] Mendes, p. 38.

[15] Lewicki, p. 20.

[16] Mendes, p. 39.

[17] *Ibid.*

[18] Lewicki, p. 197.

[19] Burton F. Beers, *World History: Patterns of Civilization*, Prentice Hall, Englewood Cliffs, New Jersey, 1990, p. 250.

[20] Robert Landry, *The Gentle Art of Flavoring*, Abelard Schuman, New York, 1970, p. 39.

[21] Constance Nabwire and Bertha Vining Montgomery, *Cooking the African Way*, Lerner Publications Co., Minneapolis, Minnesota, 1988, pp. 41, 10.

[22] Mendes, p. 43.

[23] Nabwire and Montgomery, p. 10.

[24] Moore, p. 78.

[25] Harris, p. *xiv*.

[26] Marvin Perry, *A History of the World*, Houghton Mifflin Co., Boston, Massachusetts, 1985, pp. 283-284.

[27] Michael Teague and Zélide Cowan, "Nil Disprandum [sic]," *American Heritage*, February 1969, vol. 20, no. 2, pp. 21, 20, 24.

[28] Langston Hughes and Milton Meltzer, *A Pictorial History of the Negro in America*,

Crown Publishers, Inc., New York, 1964, p. 10.

[29] James A. Rawley, *The Translantic Slave Trade*, W.W. Norton & Company, New York, 1981, p. 296.

[30] Colin Palmer, "The Cruelest Commerce," *National Geographic*, September 1992, p. 80.

[31] Rawley, pp. 292, 296-297.

[32] Palmer, p. 87.

[33] Harris, pp. *xv*, 30.

[34] Hughes and Meltzer, p. 10.

[35] Karen Hess, in Mary Randolph, *The Virginia House-Wife*, 1824 edition, reprinted as a facsimile with historical notes and commentaries by Karen Hess, University of South Carolina Press, Columbia, South Carolina, 1984, p. *xxx*.

[36] Walter Buehr, *Home Sweet Home in the Nineteenth Century*, Thomas Y. Crowell Co., New York, 1965, pp. 25, 27.

[37] Susan Kirkman Vaughn, *Life In Alabama*, manuscript submitted for Alabama textbook adoption, History Department, State Teachers College, Florence, Alabama, c. 1935, pp. 89, 93, 86, 94, 95, from the

Alabama Collection, Julia Tutwiler Library, Livingston University, Livingston, Alabama.

[38] *Ibid.*, pp. 89-90.

[39] George Schaun and Virginia C. Schaun, *Everyday Life in Colonial Virginia*, Greenberry Publications, Annapolis, Maryland, 1960, p. 59.

[40] Charles L. Perdue, Jr., Thomas E. Barden, and Robert K. Phillips, ed., *Weevils In The Wheat: Interviews with Virginia Ex-Slaves*, University Press of Virginia, Charlottesville, Virginia, 1976, p. 228, interview of Levi Pollard, Richmond, Virginia. (Note: Mr. Pollard was born c. 1850 and had lived in Charlotte County, Virginia.) The "hind" mentioned by Pollard may be a shank portion of meat, or a fish of the grouper family.

[41] The Federal Writers' Project of the Works Progress Administration (FWP/WPA), compiled 1941, *Mississippi Narratives*, vol. 9, p. 38, interview of Charlie Davenport, age 100, Natchez, Mississippi, interviewed by Edith Wyatt Moore.

[42] Henry Clay Bruce, *The New Man: Twenty-nine Years A Slave, Twenty-nine Years A*

Free Man, P. Anstadt & Sons, York, Pennsylvania, 1895, p. 61.

[43] Perdue, Barden, and Phillips, p. 154, interview of Susan Jackson, Fredericksburg, Virginia, interviewed by Marietta Silver.

[44] John W. Blassingame, editor, *Slave Testimony: Two Centuries of Letters, Speeches, Interviews, and Autobiographies*, Louisiana State University Press, Baton Rouge, Louisiana, 1977, p. 133, quoting from "Narrative of James Curry, A Fugitive Slave," *The Liberator*, January 10, 1840.

[45] Gerald Schwartz, editor, *A Woman Doctor's Civil War*, University of South Carolina Press, Columbia, South Carolina, 1984, p. 142.

[46] Solomon Northup, *Twelve Years A Slave: Narrative of Solomon Northup, A Citizen of New-York, Kidnapped in Washington City in 1841, and Rescued in 1853, From a Cotton Plantation Near the Red River, in Louisiana*, Derby & Miller, Auburn, New York, 1853, p. 169.

[47] Jno. S. Wilson, M.D., "The Negro. — His Diet, Clothing, &c.," *The American Cotton Planter and Soil of the South*, vol. 3, no. 6,

June 1859, p. 197. John Stainback Wilson was also a medical columnist for *Godey's Lady's Book and Magazine*.

[48] Kenneth M. Stampp, *The Peculiar Institution: Slavery in the Ante-Bellum South*, Vintage Books, New York, 1956, p. 284.

[49] B.A. Botkin, ed., *Lay My Burden Down*, University of Chicago Press, Chicago, Illinois, 1945, p. 84.

[50] Schwartz, pp. 69, 70.

[51] Perdue, Barden, Phillips, p. 3, interview of Mrs. Armaci Adams (b. 1859), Hampton, Virginia, interviewed June 25, 1937 by Frances Greene and Claude W. Anderson.

[52] *Ibid.*, p. 304, interview of Uncle Bacchus White, Fredericksburg, Virginia, interviewed in the fall of 1939 by Sue K. Gordon.

[53] Bruce, p. 26.

[54] Joe Gray Taylor, *Eating, Drinking, and Visiting in the South: An Informal History*, Louisiana State University Press, Baton Rouge, Louisiana, 1982, p. 90.

[55] "Agricultural Department. 1. — Management of Negroes," *De Bow's Review*,

March 1851, p. 326.

[56] FWP/WPA, *Georgia Narratives*, vol. 4, part 1, pp. 203-204, interview of Willis Cofer, age 78, Athens, Georgia, interviewed by Grace McCune.

[57] *Ibid.*, p. 146, interview of Julia (Aunt Sally) Brown, Atlanta, Georgia, interviewed July 25, 1939, by Geneva Tonsill.

[58] Ruth Coder Fitzgerald, *A Different Story: A Black History of Fredericksburg, Stafford and Spotsylvania, Virginia*, Unicorn, 1979, p. 10.

[59] Ronald Killion and Charles Waller, editors, *Slavery Time When I Was Chillun Down on Master's Plantation*, The Beehive Press, Savannah, Georgia, 1973, p. 128.

[60] Bruce, p. 17.

[61] *Georgia Narratives*, vol. 4, part 2, p. 223, interview of Charlie Hudson, age 80, Athens, Georgia, interviewed c. May 22, 1938, by Sadie B. Hornsby.

[62] FWP/WPA, *Virginia Narratives*, vol. 17, p. 45, interview of Simon Stokes, Guinea, Virginia, interviewed c. April 14, 1937, by Lucille B. Jayne.

[63] *Georgia Narratives*, vol. 4, part 1, p. 291, interview of Benny Dillard, age 80, Athens, Georgia, interviewed by Grace McCune.

[64] *Ibid.*, p. 4, interview of Rachel Adams, age 78, Athens, Georgia, interviewed by Sadie B. Hornsby.

[65] *Georgia Narratives*, vol. 4, part 3, pp. 248-249, interview of Robert Shepherd, age 91, Athens, Georgia, interviewed by Grace McCune.

[66] Bruce, p. 14.

[67] Fussell, p. 149.

[68] Moore, p. 74.

[69] *Georgia Narratives*, vol. 4, part 1, p. 47, interview of Georgia Baker, age 87, Athens, Georgia, interviewed by Sadie B. Hornsby.

[70] *Georgia Narratives*, vol. 4, part 2, p. 228, interview of Charlie Hudson, age 80, Athens, Georgia, interviewed c. May 22, 1938, by Sadie B. Hornsby.

[71] Killion and Waller, p. 40, interview of Cicely Cawthon, Toccoa, Georgia.

[72] Eugene D. Genovese, *Roll, Jordan, Roll: The World The Slaves Made*, Pantheon Books, New York, 1974, pp. 548, 547.

[73] Ethel Dixon, *Big Mama's Old Black Pot Recipes*, Stoke Gabriel Enterprises, Inc., Alexandria, Louisiana, 1987, p. 40.

[74] Frances D. and Peter J. Robotti, *French Cooking in the New World: Louisiana Creole and French-Canadian Cuisine*, Doubleday & Co., Inc., Garden City, New York, 1976, p. 392.

[75] Hughes and Meltzer, p. 163.

[76] FWP/WPA, *South Carolina Narratives*, vol. 14, part 1, p. 291, interview of Lizzie Davis, age 70 to 80, Marion, South Carolina, interviewed December 13, 1937, by Annie Ruth Davis.

[77] Robert Q. Mallard, *Plantation Life Before Emancipation*, Whittet & Shepperson, Richmond, Virginia, 1892, p. 18.

[78] Moore, p. 81.

[79] Jane Eddington, "Some Rice (Du Riz)," *Dallas Morning News*, Dallas, Texas, April 5, 1912.

[80] Mrs. V.D. Covington, "Southern Housekeeping," *The Bennington Banner*, Bennington, Vermont, July 1, 1880.

[81] Ann Parks Marshall, editor, *Martha*

Washington's Rules for Cooking, first published in the 1920s, George Washington Bicentennial Edition published in 1931, p. 139. Ann Parks Marshall included the recipe as being from the "Deep South" (rather than Virginia) — it is unclear where Bay Brook was, but she was writing about her family connections in the Arkansas/Louisiana area.

[82] G.W. [George Washington] Carver, *How to Grow the Peanut and 105 Ways of Preparing it for Human Consumption*, Bulletin No. 32, Second Edition, May 1917, Tuskegee Normal and Industrial Institute, Tuskegee, Alabama, p. 17.

[83] Perdue, Barden, Phillips, pp. 102-103, interview of Cornelius Garner (b. 1846 in Saint Mary's County, Maryland), interviewed May 18, 1937, by Emmy Wilson and Claude W. Anderson.

[84] South Carolina Division of Tourism, Columbia, South Carolina.

[85] *The Colored American*, Augusta, Georgia, December 30, 1865.

[86] *The National Leader*, Washington, D.C., December 8, 1888.

[87] Lillie S. Lustig, S. Claire Sondheim, and Sarah Rensel, editors, *The Southern Cook Book of Fine Old Recipes*, Culinary Arts Press, Reading, Pennsylvania, 1939, p. 7.

[88] Célestine Eustis, *Cooking in Old Créole Days*, R.H. Russell, New York, 1903, p. 23, recipe attributed to "Uncle John," Chef of Mr. LeGaree, of South Carolina.

[89] *Ibid.*, p. 28.

[90] Harris, p. 151.

[91] Maria Massey Barringer, *Dixie Cookery*, Loring, Publisher, Boston, Massachusetts, 1867, pp. 17-18, 28.

[92] South Carolina Division of Tourism, Columbia, South Carolina.

[93] Mrs. Mary Randolph, *The Virginia Housewife: or, Methodical Cook, Stereotype Edition, with Amendments and Additions*, Plaskitt & Cugle, Baltimore, Maryland, 1828, p. 111.

[94] G.W. [George Washington] Carver, *How to Cook Cow Peas*, Bulletin No. 13, Revised and Reprinted, Tuskegee Normal and Industrial Institute, Tuskegee, Alabama, 1908, pp. 5, 6.

[95] Randolph, *The Virginia Housewife*, p. 81.

[96] G.W. [George Washington] Carver, *How to Grow the Tomato and 115 Ways to Prepare it for the Table*, Bulletin No. 36, April 1918, Tuskegee Normal and Industrial Institute, Tuskegee, Alabama, pp. 32 and 13.

[97] Fitzgerald, p. 219.

[98] *The Elevator*, San Francisco, California, August 24, 1872.

[99] Perdue, Barden, Phillips, p. 306, interview of Uncle Bacchus White, Fredericksburg, Virginia, interviewed during the fall of 1939 by Sue K. Gordon.

[100] Karen Hess, editor, *The Carolina Rice Kitchen: The African Connection*, University of South Carolina Press, Columbia, South Carolina, 1992, pp. 96, 97.

[101] *Ibid.*, pp. 102-103.

[102] Recipe courtesy of McIlhenny Tabasco Company.

[103] Perdue, Barden, and Phillips, p. 181, interview of Beverly Jones, Gloucester Court House, Virginia, interviewed by William T. Lee.

[104] Lustig, Sondheim, and Rensel, p. 30.

[105] Eustis, *Cooking in Old Creole Days*, p. 53.

[106] Courtney Allyne, "Aunt Milly's Mush Muffins," *Housekeepers' Weekly*, December 24, 1892, p. 12.

[107] Clement Wood, "What Alabama Offers," *Arkansas Gazette*, Little Rock, Arkansas, January 13, 1924.

[108] *The Elevator*, San Francisco, California, January 25, 1873.

[109] "In the Kitchen," *Housekeeper's Weekly*, Philadelphia, Pennsylvania, May 10, 1890, p. 15. The recipe was originally called "A Maryland 'Jim Crow.' "

[110] Randolph, *The Virginia Housewife*, 1828, pp. 120-121.

[111] Recipe courtesy Manfred E. Roehr, Colonial Williamsburg chef (as printed in The Virginia Chefs Association, *The Great Chefs of Virginia Cookbook*, The Donning Company, Norfolk/Virginia Beach, Virginia, 1987, p. 127).

[112] "Help for House Wives," *The Kansas Baptist Herald*, Topeka, Kansas, March 16, 1912.

[113] Eustis, *Cooking in Old Creole Days*, p. 67.

[114] Lustig, Sondheim, and Rensel, p. 42.

[115] "The Peanut as an Article of Food," *Arthur's Home Magazine*, October 1884, p. 594.

[116] Recipe courtesy USDA.

[117] "Peach Pies," *Freedom's Journal*, New York City, New York, September 12, 1828.

[118] "Help for House Wives," *The Kansas Baptist Herald*.

Index

Ackee 8
Adams, Armaci 102
Adams, Rachel 104
Adultery 5
African 10, 13, 41
African Main Dish Peanut Butter Sauce 41
African-Style Chicken Stew 56
Alabama Baked Cow Peas (Delicious) 64
Alabama Fare 79
À la Daube 16
Alcohol 81
Ambrosia 81
Andirons 17
Animal Fat 8
Another Way to Make Hoecakes 76
Apples 8, 10, 36
Apron 36, 37
Ashcake 33
Asparagus 72
Atlantic Trade 7
Aunt Dinah 45
Aunt Hannah 22
Aunt Milly 77, 78
Aunt Milly's Mush Muffins 77
Aunt Viney 33, 34

Bacon 25-27, 39

Baker, Georgia 104
Banana Leaves 37
Barbecue 8, 68
Baskets 20, 21
Bay Brook 46
Bean(s) 4, 10, 14, 71, 80, 87
Beans and Rice 74
Beef 8, 25, 27
Beer 11, 36, 37
Bell 22
Bellows 18
Berry Cobbler 68
Big House 17
Bight of Benin 15
Biscuit(s) 29, 32, 39, 68, 80, 81
Bitterleaf 7
Black-Betty 74
Black-Eyed Peas 2, 4, 15, 71, 74
Boil Dinner 20
Boiled Pigs' Feet 61
Bosman, a Dutchman 7
Bread(s) 3, 18, 23, 27, 29, 31, 32, 34, 49, 81, 86, 90
Breakfast 20, 21, 23, 32
Broad Bean 4
Brown, Julia (Aunt Sally) 103
Brown Rice 46, 47

Bruce, Henry Clay 21, 27, 30, 34
Brunson's Station 44
Brush 17
Bucket(s) 20, 22
Butler 17
Butter 8, 29, 31
Buttermilk 21, 23, 29, 34

Cabbage Leaves 37, 38
Cabbage Rolls 38
Cabin(s) 22, 24, 27, 79
Cake(s) 10, 18, 22, 36, 37, 39, 68, 86, 87, 88-90, 91
Cake, Chocolate 68
Cake, Coconut 68
Cake, Lady Baltimore 68, 81
Cake, Marble 68
Cake, Molasses 90
Cake, Pinto Bean 87
Cake, Pork Fruit 89
Cake, Sweet and Spicy Pork 88
Cakebread 32
Cakes, Philadelphia Groundnut 91
Camel 8
Canada 38
Candies 10, 87
Candy, Peanut 93
Cannibalism 5
Carolina Pigs' Feet 60
Carver, Dr. George Washington 40, 49

Cassava 6, 7, 10
Catfish 49
Cawthon, Cicely 104
Celebration 35
Chicken(s) 6, 9, 26, 27, 36, 37, 68, 80
Chicken, Fried 80
Chicken Gumbo 54
Chicken, Soul on Rice 47
Chickpea 4
Child(ren) 17, 18, 22, 23, 25, 31-36
Chimney 19
Chitterlings 1
Chitterlings, Fried 62
Christmas 35, 36
Churn 23
Cistern 18
Civil War 38
Coals 18, 22, 30
Cobbler 68
Coconut 7, 8, 10
Cofer, Willis 29, 103
Coffee 26, 35, 39, 80, 81
Collard Greens with Ham Hocks 71
Collards 72
Columbian Exchange 7
Columbus, Christopher 6
Communal Cooking 22
Congo Bean 4
Congo Fish/American Version 48
Congris 74
Cook(s) 17-19, 22, 28, 37, 38, 39, 44, 45

Cookies, Peanut Butter 93
Cooking Facilities 22
Cooking Forks 18
Cooking Vessels 45
Cormantyn Apples 10
Corn 21, 23, 26, 27
Cornbread, Corn Bread 1,
    20, 23, 29, 32-35, 68
Corn Cakes 15
Corncrib 26
Cornmeal 10, 25
Cornpone(s), Corn Pone
    21, 29, 32, 37, 80
Corn Shuckings 35, 37
Cotton 21
Coush-Coush 35
Covington, Mrs. V.D. 44
Cowpea(s) 2, 4, 39, 64, 74
Cows 23
Cranes 18, 29
Cream 23
Creole 16, 58
Creole Jambalaya 58
Crowder Peas 74
Cuba 16
Cucumber(s) 2, 7, 8
Curry, James 22
Custard Apples 10

Dairy House 29
Dalila, Nzingha 1, 96
Dates 8
Davenport, Charlie 100
Davis, Lizzie 38, 105
Daylight 21
Diet 22, 25, 28, 30

Dillard, Benny 31, 104
Dining Room 17
Dinner 20, 23
Dinner Trays 21
Dioscorea 4
Dishes 19
Dishpan 19
Djambi 4
Doctor 13
Dogs 30
Dressing (Turkey) 68
Dubie 68
Ducks 36
Dukhn 3
Dumplings 37
Dutch Ovens 18

East Africa 8
Eddington, Jane 43
Eggplant 2, 69
Egg-Plant, How to Cook
    69
Eggs 9, 10, 26, 35, 38
Eustis, Célestine 57

Fat Back 39
Feasting 35
Fertility 5
Field 22
Field Peas 26, 63, 74
Fig Bananas 8, 9, 10
Fig Jelly 81
Figs 8
Fire 24
Fireplace(s) 17, 18, 22, 27,
    29, 31, 33, 37, 45

– 113 –

Fish 8, 15, 16, 30, 49, 68
Fish, Congo/American
  Version 48
Fishing 30, 32
Florida 16
Flour 10, 14, 29, 35
Fly Brush 17
Foodways 3, 68
Forks 18
Fouto 9
Fowl 18
French Canadian 38
French Toast, Poor Man's
  82
Fried Chitterlings 62
Fried Frog Legs 53
Fried Okra 67
Fried Oysters 52
Fritter 3
Frog Legs, Fried 53
Fruit 26, 82
Fruit Cake 89
Fufu 6, 9, 10, 48

Game 8, 32, 36
Garbanzos 4
Garden 26, 32, 33, 72
Garner, Cornelius 49, 106
Geese 36
Gelatin 16
Genius 38
George Washington
  Carver's Mock
  Chicken 49
Georgia 31
Goat 8

Gourds 2
Gout 25
Grape Leaves 38
Grapes 96
Gravy 31, 44, 45, 71
Gravy for Rice 44
Green Peppers 9
Greens 31, 32, 71, 72, 80,
  81
Greens Another Way 72
Groundnut(s) 2, 7, 10, 91,
  92
Groundpeas 32
Guinea 6, 7, 9, 15
Guinea Corn 2
Guinea Hens 9
Gumbo 1, 16, 53, 54
Gumbo, Chicken 54
Gumbo, Harlem (Stewed
  Mackerel) 53

Ham(s) 27, 35
Ham Hocks 38, 71
Harlem Gumbo (Stewed
  Mackerel) 53
Hasty Sweet Potato Pie 86
Hazelnuts 7
Heads 27
Hearth 18, 29
Hens 37
Herbal Tea 39
Herbs 38
Herring 23
Hickory Bark 29
Hind 20
Hispañola 6

Hocks 38, 71
Hoe Cake, 31, 75
Hog(s) 25, 27
Hog-Killing 35
Hominy 25, 31
Honey 39
Honey Water 11
Hooks 18, 37
Hopping John 74
Hops 30
Horn 21, 33, 34
Horse Bean 14
Hot Peppers 7
"How to Cook Egg-Plant."
    69
Hudson, Charlie 103, 104
Hunting 30, 32

Ibo 5, 6
Icie, the Cook 37
Irish Potatoes 26
Ironing 24
Iron Rods 18

Jackson, Susan 22, 101
Jambalaya 58
Jelly, Crab-Apple 81
Jollof Rice 10
Jones, Beverly 108
Jowls 27

Kettles 18
Kidney Bean 4
Kitchen 17-19, 22, 37, 44

Lady Baltimore Cake 68,
    81
Lamb 8
Lard 14, 39
LeGaree, Mr., of South
    Carolina 57
Legumes (also see Beans)
    2, 74
Lemons 15
Lentils 4
Light Bread, Lightbread
    29, 36
Lima Bean 4
Limes 15
Locust Beer 36, 37
Long Sweetening 80
Lordnorth, Marse 35
Louisiana 35
Lunch 21
Luxuries 35
Lye 31

Mackerel 53
Maids 17
Maize 2, 6, 7, 14
Mali 4
Mallard, Robert Q. 38
Mam Jinks 46
Mash 9
Mead 11
Meal 27, 49
Meals 24, 25, 28
Meat 6, 10, 15, 18, 23, 29,
    31, 32, 36, 37, 49
Melon Seeds 7
Mess of Greens 72

Middlings 27
Milk 11, 20, 23, 25, 29, 31, 32
Millet 2, 3, 11
Milling 29
Mint Julep 81
Missouri 21, 30
Mock Chicken, George Washington Carver's 49
Modern Sweet Potato Pudding 84
Molasses 20, 25, 49, 80, 90
Molasses Cake 90
Muffins, Aunt Milly's Mush 77
Muscadine (Wine) 81
Mush 14, 20
Mussel Shells 31
Mustard Greens 72
Mutton 25

New Orleans 43, 58
New Orleans Rice 43
New Potatoes with Salt Pork 70
New World Colonies 12
New World Foods 7
New Yam 5
Nigeria 5
Njam 4
North Carolina 22
Nutrition 14, 28
Nyami 4

Ochra [Okra] and Tomatos [Tomatoes] 65
Okra 2, 7, 9, 65, 67, 81
Okra, Fried 67
Okra, Stewed 81
Onion 7, 21
Onions, Boiled 80
Opossum(s) 31, 32, 80
Oven(s) 18, 29, 30, 33
Overseer(s) 21, 26
Oysters 52
Oysters, Fried 52
Oysters, Panned 52
Oyster Shells 31
Oyster Soup 51

Pail 23
Palm Wine 11
Pancake 3
Panned Oysters 52
Parch 27
Partridge à la "Uncle John" 89
Pea(s) 2, 4, 15, 26, 32, 33, 63, 64, 71, 72, 74
Peach(es) 36, 94
Peach Pie 94
Peacock Feathers 17
Peanut(s) 40, 91-93
Peanut Butter Sauce, African Main Dish 41
Peanut Butter Cookies 93
Peanut Candy 93
Peanut Soup 40
Pecans 36, 40

Peppermint Balls 36
Pepper Pot 16
Peppers 7, 9
Persimmons 31
Persimmon Beer 36
Persimmon Bread 81
Philadelphia Groundnut
    Cakes 91
Pie(s) 68, 81, 86, 87, 94,
    95
Pie, Delicious Grape 95
Pie, Hasty Sweet Potato 86
Pie, Molasses 81
Pie, Peach 94
Pig Parts 68
Pigs' Feet, Boiled 61
Pigs' Feet, Carolina 60
Pinto Bean Cake 87
Pistachios 7
Plantains 6, 8
Plums 8
Poke Salad 68, 73
Poke Salad (or "Sallet") 73
Pollard, Levi 100
Pomegranates 8
Pone(s) (also see
    Cornpone) 21, 29, 80
Poor Man's French Toast
    82
Pork Fruit Cake 89
Porridge 3, 14
Portugal 12
Portuguese Explorers 12
Possum(s) (also see
    Opossum) 31, 32, 80

Pot(s) 18, 19, 28, 29, 33,
    37
Potato(es) 7, 10, 21, 23,
    26, 31-33, 37, 39, 40,
    45, 68, 70, 80, 83, 84,
    86
Potatoes, New, with Salt
    Pork 70
Potato Salad 68
Pothook 19
Pot Liquor (also Pot
    Likker, etc.) 22, 32,
    34, 80
Poultry 8, 9, 26
Pound Cake 86
Preserves, Fig 81
Preserves, Quince 81
Pudding(s) 3, 9, 10, 84, 86
Pudding, Modern Sweet
    Potato 84
Pudding, Sweet-Potato,
    Circa 1830 84
Pumpkins 2

Quince 81

Rabbit 32
Raisins 36
Ram's Meat 6
Randolph, Mary 63
Ration(s) 25, 26, 29
Red Peas 74
Rice 2, 3, 6, 9, 10, 15, 26,
    38, 39, 43-45, 47, 48,
    74, 81

Rice, Deep South Brown 46
Rice, New Orleans 43
Rice with Fruit 82
Roasting 37
Roots 2

Salad 68, 73
Sallet 73
Salt Pork 25, 70, 88
Santee Catfish Stew 49
Sauce 3, 38
Sausage 38
Scuppernong (Wine) 81
Scurvy 14, 26
Seasoning 38
Second Cook 17
Seeds 7
Sesame Oil 8
Sesame Seeds 7
Shamwell, Jeannette Wright 68
Shea Butter 8
Sheep 27
Shells, Mussel 31
Shells, Oyster 31
Shepherd, Robert 104
Ships 12
Shortening Bread 90
Shorts 29
Short'nin Bread 90
Shoulders 27
Shovel 18
Shuckings 35
Sink 19
Skillet 18, 28

Slabber-Sauce 14
Slave Raiding Parties 11
Slavers 12, 13
Slave Trade 11
Smokehouse 26, 29
Snap Beans 80
Sorghum 2, 3, 25
Soul on Rice Chicken 47
Soup 10, 20, 40, 51, 68
Soup, Oyster 51
Soup, Peanut 40
Soup, Tuskegee Institute Tomato and Okra 66
South Carolina 38, 44, 57
Sow-Belly 80
Spanish Florida 16
Spinach 7
Spit 18
Spoons 18, 31
Spring 18
Squash 21
Starchy Grains 2
Starved 27
Stew 9, 10, 38, 49, 56, 68
Stew, African-Style Chicken 56
Stew, Santee Catfish 49
Stew, Terrapin 57
Stokes, Simon 103
Stoves 29, 44
String Beans 80
Sugar 26, 35
Sugar Cane 10, 12
Sugar Plantations 12
Sunday Bread 29
Supper 20-23

Surgeons 13
Sweetening 80
Sweet and Spicy Pork
    Cake 88
Sweetgum Trees 31
Sweet Potato(es) 6, 10, 26,
    31, 37, 39, 40, 45, 83,
    84, 86
Sweet Potato Pudding 84
Syllabub 81
Syrup 10, 32

Tamarind 8
Tapioca 10
Taters 21, 32, 33
Terrapin Stew 57
Tomatoes 7, 81
Tongs 18
Tools 18
Trapping 30
Trays 21
Trough 33, 34
Tubs 14
Turkeys 36
Turnip Greens 31, 72, 80,
    81
Turtle (also see Terrapin)
    68
Tuskegee Institute Tomato
    and Okra Soup 66

Uncle John 57, 58
Utensils 25

Vegetable(s) 15, 23, 25,
    28, 33, 34, 37, 39, 72,
    80
Vessels 45
Vicia Faba 4
Victuals 34
Virginia 27
Virginia Housewife, The
    63

Washing 24
Water 11
Watermelon 7
Well 18
West Africa 2, 4, 8, 9, 10,
    12, 58
West Indies 12, 16
Wheat 29
Whip-or-Will Peas 74
White, Bacchus 27, 72,
    102, 108
White Potato 7
Windward Coast 15
Wine, Muscadine 81
Wine, Scuppernong 81
Wood, Clement 79
Wooden Bowls 31, 32
Wooden Spoons 14, 31

Yam(s) 2, 4, 5, 6, 10, 15,
    81, 83
Yams, Yummy 83
Yeast 29
Yoruba 6
Yummy Yams [Sweet
    Potatoes] 83

Mitchells Publications

Other related titles by Patricia B. Mitchell:

Plantation Row Slave Cabin Cooking

Christmas Season During Slavery Times

Waking Up Down South

Southern Born and BREAD

Specialties from the Southern Garden

Real South Cooking

Simply Scrumptious Southern Sweets

Delightful Dreams of Dixie Dinners

Magic in the Pot

Good Food, Good Folks, Good Times

Mammy: The Hand that Rocked the South

To see more titles from Mitchells Publications, please visit *FoodHistory.com* and *MitchellsPublications.com*